Village® Country Style



A Wallpaper Playbook for Interior Design

Village® Absolutely Vintage

Schiffer Publishing Ltd®

4880 Lower Valley Road, Atglen, PA 19310 USA

# A Wallpaper Playbook for Interior Design

## COUNTRY

Tina Skinner &
FSC Wallcoverings

Village® Country Style

**Editorial Staff:**
Tina Skinner
Sabeen Khan
Melissa Cardona
Nathaniel Wolfgang-Price

**Technical Advisors:**
Kathy O'Brien
Fred Dodnick

**Photography:**
Melissa Cardona

**Cover Design & Layout:**
John P. Cheek

Library of Congress Cataloging-in-Publication Data

Skinner, Tina.
A wallpaper playbook for interior design : country / by Tina Skinner & F. Schumacher & Co.
p. cm.
ISBN 0-7643-2170-6 (hardcover)
1. Wallpaper. 2. Decoration and ornament, Rustic. 3. F. Schumacher & Co. I. F. Schumacher & Co. II. Title.

NK3399.S56 2005
745.54—dc22
2004028003



Type set in Americana BT/Souvenir Lt BT

ISBN: 0-7643-2170-6
Printed in China

Published by Schiffer Publishing Ltd.
4880 Lower Valley Road
Atglen, PA 19310
Phone: (610) 593-1777; Fax: (610) 593-2002
E-mail: Info@schifferbooks.com

For the largest selection of fine reference books on this and related subjects, please visit our web site at **www.schifferbooks.com**
We are always looking for people to write books on new and related subjects.
If you have an idea for a book please contact us at the above address.

This book may be purchased from the publisher. Include $3.95 for shipping.
Please try your bookstore first. You may write for a free catalog.

In Europe, Schiffer books are distributed by
Bushwood Books
6 Marksbury Ave.
Kew Gardens
Surrey TW9 4JF England
Phone: 44 (0) 20 8392-8585; Fax: 44 (0) 20 8392-9876
E-mail: info@bushwoodbooks.co.uk
Free postage in the U.K., Europe; air mail at cost.

Gramercy® Nature's Orchard

Gramercy® Garden Elements

FSC Wallcoverings®

A DIVISION OF F. SCHUMACHER & CO.

## — Acknowledgments —

For information, please contact us:

FSC Wallcoverings
79 Madison Avenue
New York, NY 10016
Customer Service: 1-800-988-7775
www.fschumacher.com



**Credits**
Front Cover: Village® Country Style

Village® Vintage Countryside

# Introduction

Wallpaper is a great choice for those planning a country theme for their home's interior. With a vast selection of colors, patterns, and textures, realizing the collected, layered look of country with wallpaper is easy.

In the home, country décor provides a retreat from the hectic bustle of modern life – far away from rush-hour traffic, high-speed modems, and the electronic pulse of the twenty-first century. Country style exudes a timeless charm by combining different patterns, textures, colors, and styles of furniture. A mix of natural materials, from wood furniture and flooring to hand-made crafts, is used to achieve the look, along with rustic décor items like old glass bottles and ceramics, straw brooms, and baskets. The end result is a casual, friendly, and unpretentious atmosphere where comfort is the ultimate goal.

Today's designers are stretching the traditional boundaries of rural style to include Tuscan, French, and British country designs. These international fusions are rich with the coziness and rustic charm that makes country style so universally appealing.

Here is an opportunity to play with different hues, textures, and motifs. Match gingham with a barnyard motif, apples with plaid, floral patterns with stripes! Let your creative juices flow as you flip through the thousands of possibilities to build those layers that most excite your eye.

There are no set rules to dictate which patterns are best mixed – only your personal, impeccable taste! The swatches shown were chosen to complement each other, and how you mix and match them is sure to draw compliments when they are combined in your home.

An eclectic collection of mugs and ceramics is the theme of this wallpaper border, which adds a rustic touch to a modern kitchen. Shown: Village® Country Club Collection

Dried flora, bows, and gingham create a charming atmosphere that evokes a simpler time.
Shown: Village® Country Style

Wallpaper gives the effect of faux-finishing, punctuated by red apples and a patriotic border.
Shown: Waverly® Country House

Pink and lavender flowers bloom year-round in this pastel yellow bedroom.
Shown: Gramercy® Elegant Home

Farm animals and pastoral scenes create a motif that continues from the kitchen into the dining room.
Shown: Village® Borders for All Around the House

Wallpaper provides the charm of stenciled walls without all the work.
Shown: Waverly® Country House

Fruit motifs are popular in both traditional and European country styling. Here, the wallpaper has a faux-finished look, giving a sense of history to the room.
Shown: Gramercy® Tuscan Country Home

A porch railing gives a Southern sensibility to this bedroom, where country charm and gentility create a casually elegant combination.
Shown: Gramercy® Restoration Collection

Roosters, weather veins, and horses make you feel like you're back on the farm.
Shown: Waverly® Country House

Birdhouses add a homey touch to this welcoming foyer.
Shown: Village® Country Style

Country goes global when grapes and vines give the impression of a Tuscan vineyard.
Shown: Gramercy® Tuscan Country Home

Pink, potted flowers bloom perpetually overhead in an airy, feminine room.
Shown: Village® Claire Murray Lifestyles

Stipes and flowers are the perfect complement to an old-fashioned footed bathtub and painted furniture.
Shown: Waverly® Family Style

Since 1889, F. Schumacher & Co. has provided distinguished products of the highest quality. Founded by Frederick Schumacher, a Parisian with an exceptional eye for fine textiles, the firm grew rapidly from a small showroom on Broadway and 22nd Street in New York City to become the foremost name in the interior furnishings industry. Schumacher has been at the forefront of design trends since its founding and has pioneered numerous experiments that later became part of American decorative history. Still owned and managed by descendants of its founder, Schumacher continues its legacy of traditional, historic, classic and contemporary designs. A premiere resource to the professional design community, Schumacher, a division of F. Schumacher & Co., continues its legacy of creating fine, high-end products that infuse style, elegance, and vitality to the rooms of today and tomorrow with a peerless selection of products.

SCHUMACHER®

A youthful, American spirit has been the hallmark of Greeff fabrics and wallpapers from the start. Founded in 1933 by Theodore Greeff, the Greeff Co. gained a reputation for high-quality handblocked prints, which it imported from England. Today, Greeff's designers have an invaluable asset in the company's famous archive. Not only is it a fund of information on period European decoration, but a storehouse of Greeff's vibrant collections from the 1940s though the 1970s enhances Greeff's expertise and stature today as an originator of outstanding American design. In 1996, F. Schumacher & Co., one of the nation's leading firms in the home furnishings industry, further expanded its product offerings and acquired Greeff. As a division within Schumacher, Greeff distributes fabric, wallcoverings, and custom home fashions to the design trade.

Greeff®

Gramercy, whose parent company is the venerable F. Schumacher & Co., offers wallpapers and fabrics designed for the style-conscious consumer with an assured taste level. Offered through fine paint and wallpaper stores, specialty retailers and interior design showrooms nationwide, Gramercy enjoys a loyal following among consumers who prefer a non-traditional look that is both distinct and livable. Fresh in its approach, Gramercy's signature look is delightfully difficult to typecast, and impossible to tire of.

GRAMERCY®

Waverly, one of the most recognized names in home furnishings, personifies attainable classic design. Its wallpapers, fabrics, decorative accessories and licensed tableware, paper products and other items are sought after for their brilliant coordination and stylish ease. Waverly, a premier lifestyle brand whose signature look is expertly translated into countless classic styles, is available through retailers and interior design showrooms nationwide.

WAVERLY®

Village wallpapers are designed for those whose priority is effortless decorating. Village offers an amazing breadth of great-looking, affordable wallpapers as well as easy-to-use wall décor accessories, including borders, appliques, and faux finish décor kits. Village also creates wallpapers and borders under exclusive licenses with worldwide brands such as Coca-Cola, NASCAR, Major League Baseball, and The National Football League.

Village®

Bandana Foulard
Collection: Village® Country Club
Pattern #5806242 Rust
Other Colorways: Forest, Khaki
Width: 20 1/2" (52cm)
Vertical Repeat: 10 1/4" (26cm)

5811938 Saffron

5811935 Ecru

---

Chef's Border
Collection: Village® Essential Kitchen and Bath 2
Other Colorways: Ecru, Café, Saffron
Height: 7" (18cm)

5807275 Red & Teastain

Village® Country Mini
Collection: Village® Country Club
Pattern #5807276 Blue & Parchment
Other Colorways: Gold & Linen, Red & Teastain
Width: 20 1/2" (52cm)
Vertical Repeat: 2 1/2" (6cm)

Floral patterned wallpaper and border add to the light and airy feeling of this kitchen. Blue gingham is the perfect accent.
Shown: Waverly® Color Resource

---

Sunflower Folk Trail
Collection: Village® Borders For All Around the House
Pattern #5810445 Parchment
Other Colorways: White
Width: 20 1/2" (52cm)
Vertical Repeat: 20 1/2 (52cm)

French Rooster Border
Collection: Village® Country Canvas
Pattern #5803491 Sage
Other Colorways: Navy & Hunter
Height: 6.875"

681380 Sage & Purple

Water Garden Border
Collection: Gramercy® Nature's Orchard
Pattern #681380 Sage & Purple
Other Colorways: Burgundy, Golden Red, Rust
Height: 9.50" (24.13cm)
Horizontal Repeat: 20.50" (52.07cm)

5807052 Wedgewood & Red

5807050 Delft Blue

---

Americana Floral Mini
Collection: Village® Liberty Home
Pattern #5807051 Red & Gold
Other Colorways: Delft Blue, Wedgewood & Red
Width: 20 1/2" (52cm)
Vertical Repeat: 3" (7cm)

204023 Red

204022 Blue

Raleigh Tavern Resist
Collection: Greeff® Williamsburg Reserve Collection
Pattern #204024 Black
Other Colorways: Ivory, Green, Blue, Red
Width: 27" (69cm)
Vertical Repeat: 11" (28cm)

202941 Corn Silk

202943 Sprig

Millington
Collection: Greeff® Portraits of America
Pattern #202944 Brick
Other Colorways: Oyster, Corn Silk, Sprig, Delft
Width: 20 1/2" (52cm)
Vertical Repeat: 19"

204583 Primary

204582 Coral

Stencil Tiles
Collection: Greeff® Salt Box House
Pattern #204580 Document
Other Colorways: Pale Blue, Coral, Primary
Width: 27"
Vertical Repeat: 12.5"

204163 Gold

204160 Red

---

Stars
Collection: Greeff® Williamsburg Reserve Collection
Pattern #204162 Mineral
Other Colorways: Black, Red Gold
Width: 27" (69cm)
Vertical Repeat: 3" (8cm)

5810657 Traditional

5810659 Blue & White

Country Heart Toss
Collection: Village® Country Style
Pattern #5810656 Navy
Other Colorways: Beige & Burgundy, Traditional, Golder
Blue & White
Width: 20 1/2" (52cm)
Vertical Repeat: 3 1/2" (9cm)

5810726 Pink

Stencil Heart Toss
Collection: Village® Country Style
Pattern #5810725 Navy
Other Colorways: Pink, Bright Blue
Width: 20 1/2" (52cm)
Vertical Repeat: 3 1/2" (9cm)

204643 Moss

Providence Resist
Collection: Greeff® Salt Box House
Pattern #204642 Rye
Other Colorways: Moss, Indigo, Cranberry
Width: 27"
Vertical Repeat: 20"

5507217 Emerald

Wynfield Manor
Collection: Waverly® Southern Charm
Pattern #5507214 Fig
Other Colorways: Scarlet, Ecru, Honeysuckle, Emerald, Onyx
Width: 27" (69cm)
Vertical Repeat: 6 7/8" (17cm)

204030 Green

204032 Red

Tiny Tulips
Collection: Greeff® Williamsburg Reserve Collection
Pattern #204033 Beige
Other Colorways: Green, Blue, Red, Black
Width: 27" (69cm)
Vertical Repeat: 1" (3cm)

204083 Gold & Indigo

204080 Blue

---

Charlotte
Collection: Greeff® Williamsburg Reserve Collection
Pattern #204082 Red
Other Colorways: Blue, Green, Gold & Indigo
Width: 20 1/2" (52cm)
Vertical Repeat: 24" (61cm)

5808351 Red

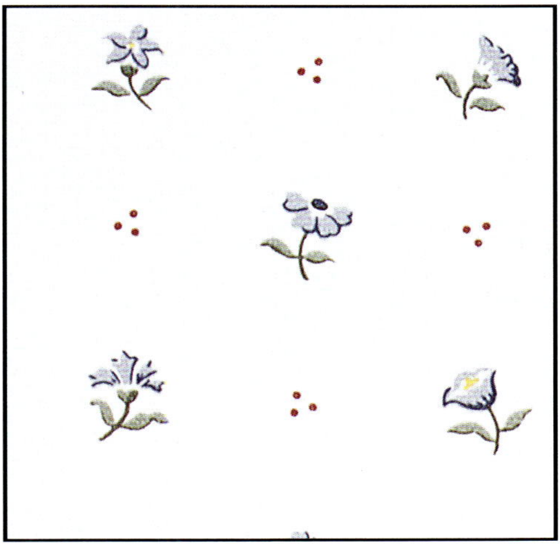

5808352 Blue

Mini Fleur Dots
Collection: Village® Claire Murray Lifestyles
Pattern #5808350 Black
Other Colorways: Blue, Red, Multi
Width: 20 1/2" (52 cm)
Vertical Repeat: 3 3/8" (9cm)

5808377 Blue

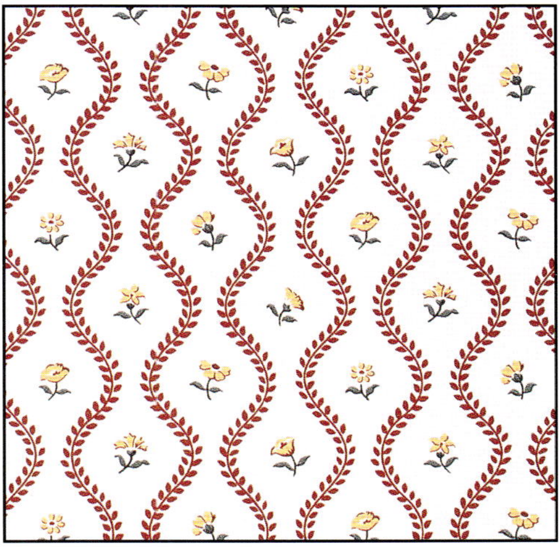

5808376 Red

Mini Fleur Stripe
Collection: Village® Claire Murray Lifestyles
Pattern #5808378 Multi
Other Colorways: Blue, Red
Width: 20 1/2" (52cm)
Vertical Repeat: 3 3/8" (9cm)

200721 Sage

200723 Blue

---

Glenmere Ticking
Collection: Greeff® Country Manor
Pattern #200720 Sand
Other Colorways: Sage, Pink, Blue
Width: 27"
Vertical Repeat: 1 1/4"

5505083 Ivory

5505082 Rose

Petals
Collection: Waverly® Atrium
Pattern #5505080 Sage
Other Colorways: Ivory, White, Rose
Width: 20 1/2" (52cm)
Vertical Repeat: 1/2" (1cm)

Country Teacup Border

5806266 Country Blue

Country Teacup Border
Collection: Village® Country Club
Pattern #5806265 Walnut
Other Colorways: Country Blue
Height: 4 5/8" (12cm)

Country Shelf Border

#5806260 Walnut

Country Shelf Border
Collection: Village® Country Club
Other Colorways: Country Blue
Height: 8 1/4" (21cm)

5502890 Jewel

Mill Grove
Collection: Waverly® Country House
Pattern #5502892 Parchment
Other Colorways: Jewel
Width: 20 1/2" (52cm)
Vertical Repeat: 27"

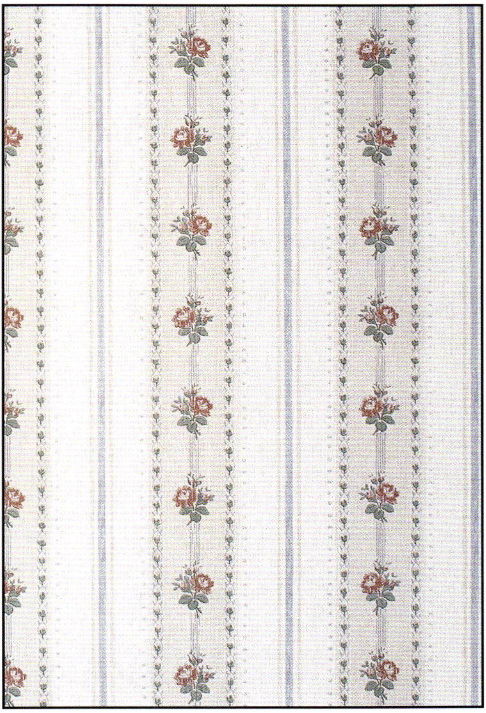

5812205 Whitewash & Blue

---

Sadie Stripe
Collection: Village® Absolutely Vintage
Pattern #5812206 Teastain & Sage
Other Colorways: Whitewash & Blue
Width: 20 7/8" (53cm)
Vertical repeat: 3 1/2" (9cm)

5806916 Antique

Apple Orchard Mini
Collection: Village® Liberty Home
Pattern #5806915 Red & White
Other Colorways: Antique
Width: 20 1/2" (52cm)
Vertical Repeat: 6 7/8" (17cm)

5502972 Slate

Apple A Day
Collection: Waverly® Country House
Pattern #5502971 Antique
Other Colorways: Slate, Candy Red
Width: 20 1/2" (52cm)
Vertical Repeat: 10 1/4"

5502503 Red

5502502 Beige

Botanical Cherry Toss
Collection: Waverly® NY Botanical Gardens
Pattern #5502500 Yellow
Other Colorways: Primary, Beige, Red
Width: 27" (69cm)
Vertical Repeat: 10 1/4" (26cm)

A wallpaper border provides interest in any room. Borders also break up vertical height to add a cozy feeling.
Shown: Waverly® Family Style

---

Colin's Folk Farm Border
Collection: Village® Borders For All Around the House
Pattern # 5810432 Black
Other Colorways: Navy, Forest & Rust
Height: 6 1/4" (16cm)

ABC
DEF

681462 Rust

681463 Golden Red

---

Ormond Texture Plaid
Collection: Gramercy® Nature's Orchard
Pattern #681460 Burgundy
Other Colorways: Plum & Teal, Rust, Golden Red, Sage
Width: 20.50" (52.07cm)
Vertical Repeat: 7" (17.78cm)

680893 Dark Sage

680892 Golden

---

Chauncey Check
Collection: Gramercy® Exclusively Yours
Pattern #680894 Blue
Other Colorways: Beige, Charcoal, Golden, Dark Sage, Red
Width: 20 1/2" (52cm)
Vertical Repeat: 10.25" (26.04 cm)

5806761 Sage

Country Orchard Plaid
Collection: Village® Home for the Weekend
Pattern #5806760 Yellow
Other Colorways: Sage
Width: 20 1/2" (52cm)
Vertical Repeat: 5 1/4" (12.7cm)

La Cloture Rustique Dado

526783 Camel

La Cloture Rustique Dado
Collection: Schumacher® Garden Pleasures
Pattern #526781 Yellow
Other Colorways: Ivory, Camel, Document, Robin's Egg,
Height: 27.25" (69cm)
Horizontal Repeat: 27.25" (69cm)

683771 Yellow

683772 Beige

Fern Trellis
Collection: Gramercy® Elegant Home
Pattern #683770 White
Other Colorways: Beige, Yellow
Width: 27" (69cm)
Vertical Repeat: 19" (48cm)

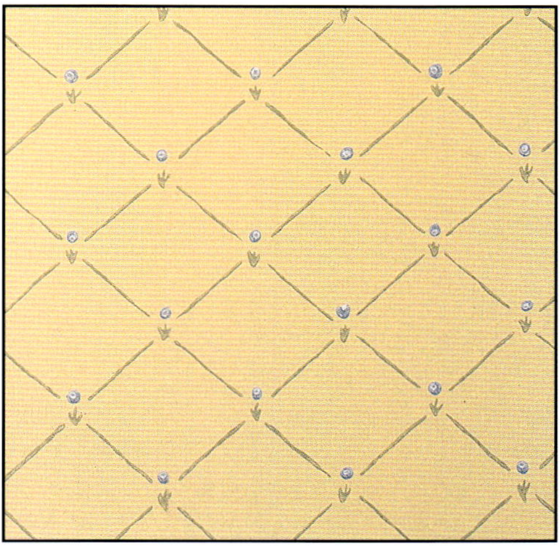

5505152 Yellow

5505154 White

Laura
Collection: Waverly® Atrium
Pattern #5505150 Green
Other Colorways: Blue, Yellow, Ivory, White
Width: 20 1/2" (52cm)
Vertical Repeat: 1 1/2" (4cm)

680002 White

Conservatory Lattice
Collection: Gramercy® Spring Fair
Pattern #680000 Sky
Other Colorways: Yellow, White, Beige, Sage
Width: 27" (68.58cm)
Vertical Repeat: 6" (15.24cm)

581649 Blue & White

5810647 Plum

---

Mini Hydrangea Trail
Collection: Village® Country Style
Pattern #5810645 Yellow
Other Colorways: Burgundy, Plum, Sage, Blue & White
Width: 20 1/2" (52cm)
Vertical Repeat: 10 1/4" (26cm)

5806515 Pink

Avignon Toss
Collection: Village® Toiles & Florals
Pattern #5806516 Yellow
Other Colorways: Lavender, Pink
Width: 21" (53cm)
Vertical Repeat: 21" (53cm)

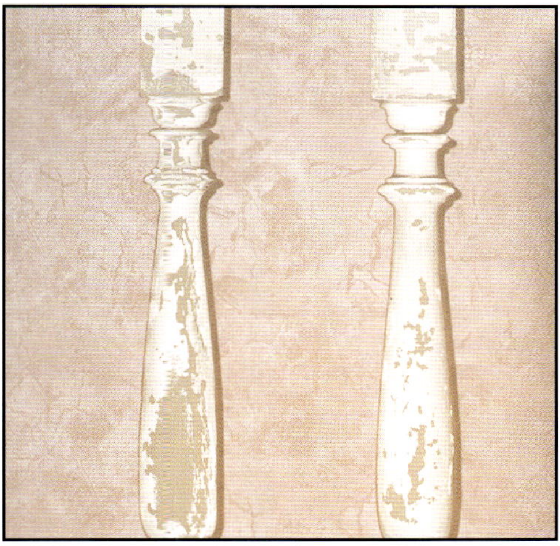

684873 Pink & Cream

684870 Green

---

Spindle Border
Collection: Gramercy® Restoration
Pattern #684872 Beige
Other Colorways: Green, Pink & Cream, Russet, Taupe
Height: 27" (69cm)
Horizontal Repeat: 20.88" (53cm)

5812161 Burgundy

5812160 Bark

---

Vintage Siding
Collection: Village® Absolutely Vintage
Pattern #5812162 Whitewash
Other Colorways: Bark, Burgundy
Width: 20 7/8" (53cm)
Vertical Repeat: 21" (53cm)

5808886 Bleached Oak

5808889 Whitewash

---

Wainscotting
Collection: Village® Liberty Home
Pattern #5808888 Sage Green
Other Colorways: Antique Gold, Bleached Oak, Wedgewood, Whitewash
Width: 20 1/2" (52cm)

204012 Blue

204010 Taupe

Delft Tiles
Collection: Greeff® Williamsburg Reserve Collection
Pattern #204013 Green
Other Colorways: Taupe, Red, Blue
Width: 27" (69cm)
Vertical Repeat: 24 1/4" (64cm)

Wallpaper dictates the color scheme in this kitchen and family room. Several variations of the same pattern make it easy to create a theme in your home's décor.
Shown: Village® Country Canvas

---

Coc-A-Doodle-Doo
Collection: Village® Essential Kitchen and Bath 2
Pattern # 5812007 Ochre & Red
Other Colorways: Blue & Sand, Sand
Width: 20 1/2" (52cm)
Vertical Repeat: 10 1/4" (26cm)

528832 Sage

Nassau Weave
Collection: Schumacher® Garden Tour
Pattern #528831 Chamois
Other Colorways: Sand, Sage, Brown
Width: 27" (68.58cm)
Vertical Repeat: 6.31" (16.03cm)

5508321 Tan

Raffia
Collection: Waverly® Colors For My Home
Pattern #5508322 Sage
Other Colorways: Beige, Tan
Width: 20 1/2" (52cm)
Vertical Repeat: 20 1/2" (52cm)

5508320 Beige

Die-cut and traditional borders are used in combination with complimentary floral and gingham patterns to break up the height of a room. Shown: Village® Borders For All Around the House

Quilting Bee Trail
Collection: Waverly® American Landscape
Pattern # 5506952 Purple
Other Colorways: Red, Navy
Width: 20 1/2" (52cm)
Vertical Repeat: 10 1/2" (27cm)

204632 Parchment

Alice Stripe
Collection: Greeff® Salt Box House
Pattern #204631 Gold
Other Colorways: Rose, Parchment
Width: 20.4"
Vertical Repeat: 15"

Country cottages line the wall and break up the vertical height of this family room.
Shown: Waverly® American Landscape

Between the Pickets Toss
Collection: Village® Home for the Weekend
Pattern # 5806795 Blue
Other Colorways: Bright
Width: 20 1/2" (52cm)
Vertical repeat: 20 7/8"

5812547 Crimson

Gabriella
Collection: Village® Silk and Satin Style
Pattern #5812546 Sorbet
Other Colorways: Navy, Crimson, Camel, Antique
Width: 20 1/2" (52cm)
Vertical Repeat: 7" (18cm)

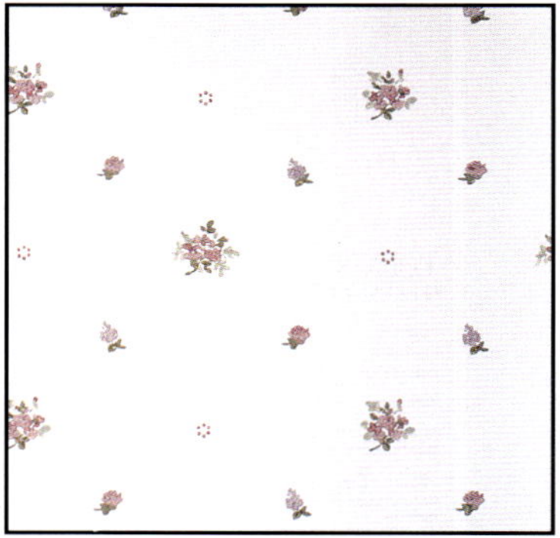

576327 Thistle

Victoria's Toss
Collection: Waverly® Country House
Pattern #576324 Country Red
Other Colorways: Colonial, Lake, Harvest, Spring, Antique, Jewel, Thistle
Width: 27"
Vertical Repeat: 12 5/8"

Botanical Trellis

5502481 Blue

Botanical Trellis
Collection: Waverly® NY Botanical Gardens
Pattern #5502480 Yellow
Other Colorways: Sage, Blue, Beige
Width: 27" (69cm)
Vertical Repeat: 10 1/4" (26cm)

5502483 Sage

680854 Gold

Amanda Leaf Trellis
Collection: Gramercy® Exclusively Yours
Pattern #680850 Moss
Other Colorways: Red, Bordeaux, Cream, Gold
Width: 20 1/2" (52cm)
Vertical Repeat: 4.19" (10.64cm)

5502341 Green on White

Ivy Vine
Collection: Waverly® NY Botanical Gardens
Pattern #5502340 Red
Other Colorways: Green on White, Yellow, Beige
Width: 27" (69cm)
Vertical Repeat: 24" (61cm)

5502342 Yellow

Trim and cabinetry were painted to match a country motif border, adding warmth and color to the bathroom. Shown: Waverly® American Landscape

American Sweetheart
Collection: Waverly® American Landscape
Pattern # 5507010 Burgundy
Other Colorways: Red, Teal
Width: 20 1/2" (52cm)
Vertical Repeat: 20 1/2" (52cm)

5503101 Sage

Garden Whisper Plaid
Collection: Waverly® There's No Place Like Home
Pattern #5503100 Blue Yellow
Other Colorways: Burgundy, Sage, Plum, Red
Width: 20 1/2" (52cm)
Vertical Repeat: 10 1/2" (27cm)

5810395 Yellow & Red

Blossom Gingham Toss
Collection: Village® Borders For All Around the House
Pattern #5810396 Pink & Purple
Other Colorways: Yellow & Red
Width: 20 1/2" (52cm)
Vertical Repeat: 10 1/4" (26cm)

A collection of blue plates is on display, adding a punch of color to a dining room hutch. Color also punctuates the table and a collection of baskets. Shown: Waverly® Family Style

Country Road Star
Collection: Village® Country Style
Pattern # 5810736 Blue
Other Colorways: Teal
Width: 20 1/2" (52cm)
Vertical Repeat: 10 1/4" (26cm)

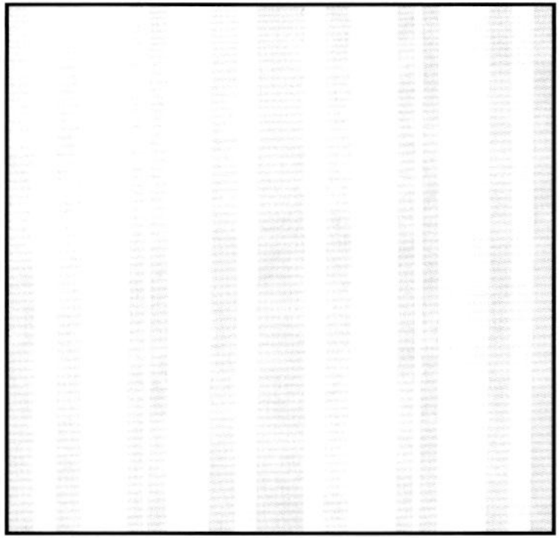

680110 Blue on White

Natalie's Plaid
Collection: Gramercy® Spring Fair
Pattern #680112 Linen
Other Colorways: Beige on Cream, Blue on White
Width: 27" (68.58cm)
Vertical Repeat: 27" (68.58cm)

## Classic Gingham

Classic Gingham
Collection: Village® Vintage Countryside
Pattern #5804760 Olive
Other Colorways: Golden, Verde, Canary, Ivory, Autumn Green, Denim, Geranium
Width: 20 1/2" (52cm)
Vertical repeat: 1/4"

## Country Fair

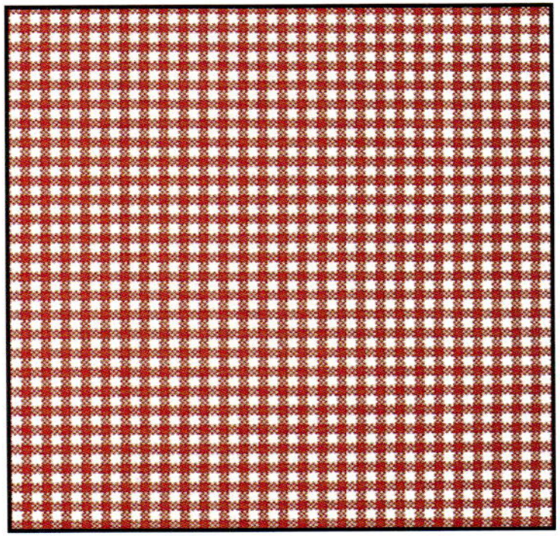

571172 Crimson

Country Fair
Collection: Waverly® Reminisce
Other Colorways: Mulberry, Indigo
Width: 27" (69cm)
Vertical Repeat: 3" (8cm)

5506113 Sage

Le Poire
Collection: Waverly® French Accent
Pattern #5506110 Porcelain
Other Colorways: Porcelain, Golden, Spice, Sage
Width: 20 1/2" (52cm)
Vertical Repeat: 20 1/2" (52cm)

5506114 Black

575673 Peach

Mistral Toss
Collection: Waverly® Country House
Pattern #575670 Red
Other Colorways: Plum, Peach, Blue, Yellow
Width: 27"
Vertical Repeat: 6 3/4"

575674 Plum

Summer Cherry Toss Plaid

680133 Linen

Summer Cherry Toss Plaid
Collection: Gramercy® Spring Fair
Pattern #680130 Primary
Other Colorways: Yellow, Cream, Linen
Width: 27" (68.58cm)
Vertical Repeat: 13.5" (34.29

680131 Yellow

5507001 Navy

Homestead Welcome Toss
Collection: Waverly® American Landscape
Pattern #5507002 Rust
Other Colorways: Red, Navy
Width: 20 1/2" (52cm)
Vertical Repeat: 5 1/8" (13cm)

5804259 Hunter

Dawn Stripe
Collection: Village® Home For The Weekend
Pattern #5808725 Blue
Other Colorways: Olive, Traditional, Navy, Khaki, Hunter
Width: 20 1/2" (52cm)

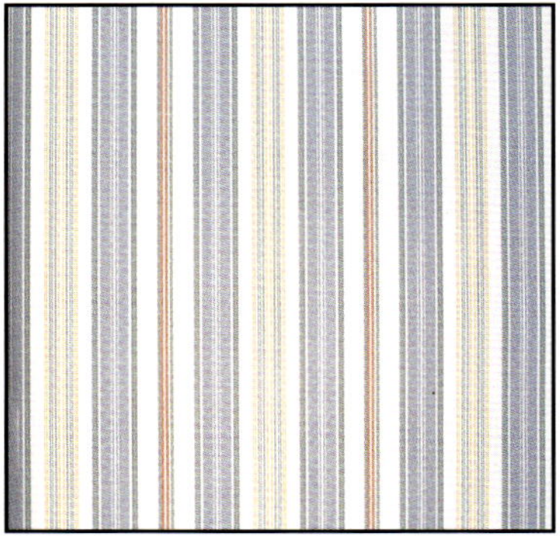

5806452 Brights

Pajama Stripe
Collection: Village® Toiles & Florals
Pattern #5806450 Dusty Plum
Other Colorways: Teastain, Brights, Basil, Sage, Lavender, Camel
Width: 21" (53cm)

5806520 Basil

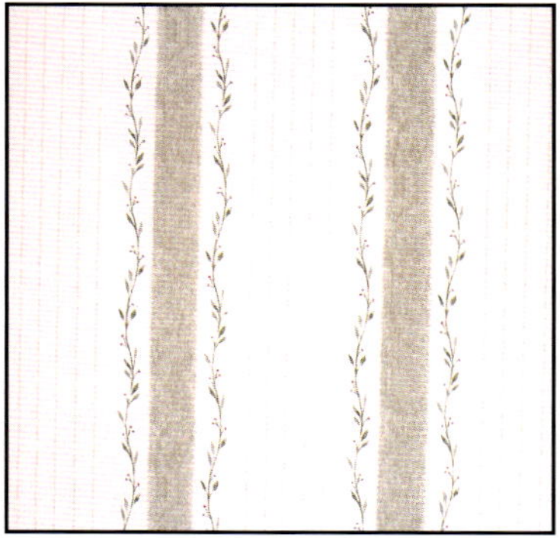

5505812 Sage

Brentwood Stripe
Collection: Waverly® American Landscape
Pattern #5505810 Black
Other Colorways: Yellow & Blue, Sage
Width: 20 1/2" (52cm)
Vertical Repeat: 7" (18cm)

5505811 Yellow & Blue

## Liberty Stripe

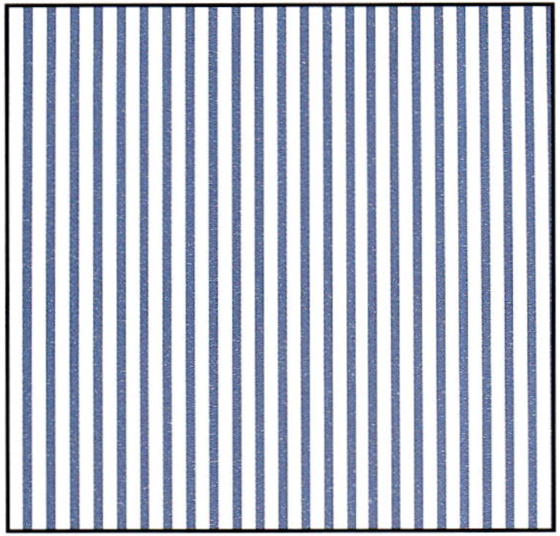

5806925 Ocean Blue

Liberty Stripe
Collection: Village® Liberty Home
Pattern #5806926 Burgundy
Other Colorways: Ocean Blue
Width: 20 1/2" (52 cm)

## Everett Stripe

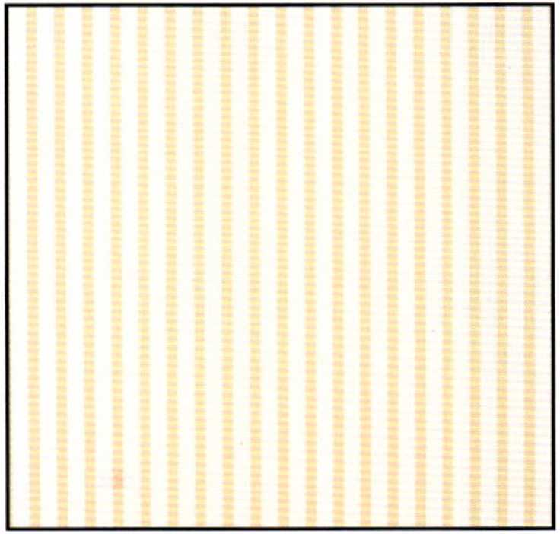

Everett Stripe
Collection: Waverly® Reminisce
Pattern #571390 Citron
Other Colorways: Jade, Teal, Lilac, Springtime
Width: 27" (69cm)

5810566 Linen & Beige

Village® Linen Stripe
Collection: Village® Borders For All Around the House
Pattern #5810565 Yellow & White
Other Colorways: Linen & Beige
Width: 20 1/2" (52cm)

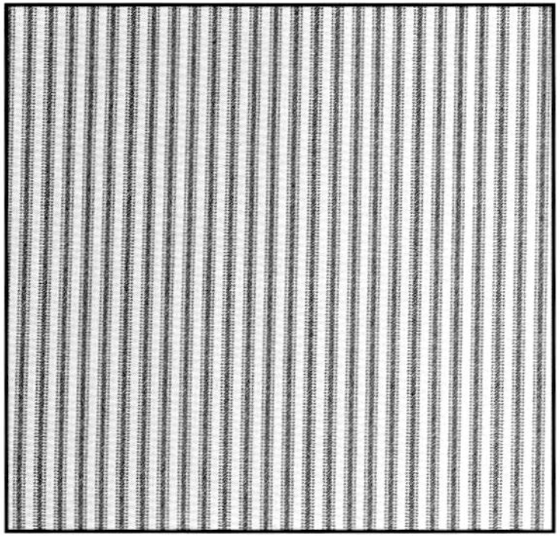

5808833 Green & White

Country Classic Ticking
Collection: Village® Liberty Home
Pattern #5808830 Teastain & Burgundy
Other Colorways: Linen & Red, Navy, Green & White
Width: 20 1/2"

575773 Yellow

La Petite Ferme
Collection: Waverly® Reminisce
Pattern #575774 Lake
Other Colorways: Sage, Blue, Yellow, Spice, Red, Black
Width: 27" (69cm)
Vertical Repeat: 18 7/8" (48cm)

5505820 Sage

Harlow Toile
Collection: Waverly® Family Style
Pattern #5505825 Red
Other Colorways: Sage, Burgundy, Navy, Black, Blue
Width: 20 1/2" (52cm)
Vertical Repeat: 20 1/2" (52cm)

5505822 Navy

A red toile pattern provides country scenery in this bedroom, where gingham and plaid textiles are used to accent the wallpaper.
Shown: Jones Toile, from the Greeff® Williamsburg Reserve Collection

Jones Toile
Collection: Greeff® Williamsburg Reserve Collection
Pattern #203994 Black
Other Colorways: Document Red, Blue, Violet, Sepia
Width: 30" (76cm)
Vertical Repeat: 63" (160cm

Roosters are a classic country motif. Here, the pattern from the kitchen's wallpaper border is used to cover the dining room's walls, creating a sense of continuity in this home's décor. Shown: Claire Murray Lifestyles, from Village®

Rooster Trellis Toile
Collection: Village® Claire Murray Lifestyles
Pattern #5808321 Red
Other Colorways: Blue, Black
Width: 20 1/2" (52cm)
Vertical Repeat: 6 7/8" (17cm)

A pastoral scene in rich, warm tones is a great choice for a dining room furnished in antiques or antique reproductions with distressed wood finishes.
Shown: Waverly® American Landscape

Hickory Landscape
Collection: Waverly® American Landscape
Pattern #5506931 Navy
Other Colorways: Burgundy
Width: 20 1/2" (52cm)
Vertical Repeat: 21" (53cm)

5502371 Yellow

Gardener's Toss
Collection: Waverly® NY Botanical Gardens
Pattern #5502370 Primary
Other Colorways: Beige, Yellow
Width: 27" (69cm)
Vertical Repeat: 18" (46cm)

548145 Celadon

Arden Texture
Collection: Gramercy® Garden Elements
Pattern #548144 Lavender
Other Colorways: Off-White, Beige, Yellow, Tan, Blue, Celadon, Red
Width: 27" (68.58cm)
Vertical Repeat: 25.25" (64.14cm)

548147 Blue

Instead of a backsplash behind the sink, this kitchen features a wallpaper border of rustic bottles that complement the bottles sitting on a display shelf. Shown: Waverly® American Landscape

Twinkle Toss
Collection: Village® Country Style
Pattern # 5806911 Cream & Navy
Other Colorways: White & Blue, Antique & Red
Width: 20 1/2" (52cm)
Vertical Repeat: 6 7/8" (18cm)

5505052 Green

Jems
Collection: Waverly® Atrium
Pattern #5505051 Yellow
Other Colorways: Blue, White, Green
Width: 20 1/2" (52cm)
Vertical Repeat: 4 1/8" (10cm)

5505051 Yellow

5507902 Mist

Rose Hill Vine
Collection: Waverly® Summer Breeze
Pattern #5507904 Crimson
Other Colorways: Lake, Sunshine, Mist, Ebony
Width: 20 1/2" (52cm)
Vertical repeat: 5 1/4" (13cm)

5507901 Sunshine

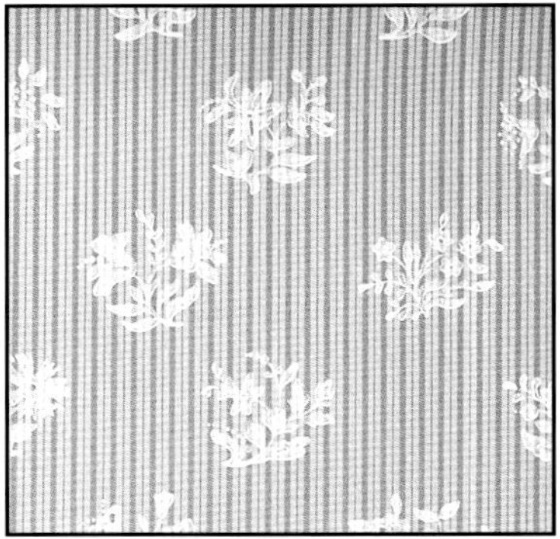

202904 Aquamarine

Martha Stencil
Collection: Greeff® Portraits of America
Pattern #202900 Gold
Other Colorways: Aquamarine, Rose, Spring Green, Delft
Width: 27"
Vertical Repeat: 6 7/8"

5810665 Burgundy

Calico Mini Vine
Collection: Village® Country Style
Pattern #5810666 Navy & Cream
Other Colorways: Burgundy, Hunter, Red, Sage
Width: 20 1/2" (52cm)
Vertical Repeat: 5 1/8" (13cm)

581667 Red

5508003 Sunshine

Garland
Collection: Waverly® Summer Breeze
Pattern #5508004 Willow
Other Colorways: Sand, Linen, Gold, Sunshine, Mist, Blue, Crimson
Width: 20 1/2" (52cm)
Vertical repeat: 5 1/8" (12.7cm)

Floral wallpaper and textiles bring to mind rolling hills of blooms in spring. In this room, the season of new life never withers away.
Shown: Waverly® Reminisce

Clarinda
Collection: Waverly® Reminisce
Pattern #5502832 Lake
Other Colorways: Colonial, Rose, Berry, Violet
Width: 27" (69cm)
Vertical Repeat: 25 1/4" (64cm)

573644 Sunshine

573640 Linen

Charming Check
Collection: Waverly® Sketchbook II
Pattern #573642 Sky
Other Colorways: Linen, Grass, Sunshine, Buttercup, Primrose
Width: 27" (69cm)
Vertical Repeat: 6 7/8" (17cm)

A pineapple border wraps around a dining room, welcoming guests and family to the dinner table. Shown: Waverly® American Landscape

Farmstead
Collection: Waverly® American Landscape
Pattern # 572065 Charcoal
Other Colorways: Indigo, Barn Red, Linen
Width: 27" (69cm)
Vertical Repeat: 13 1/2" (34cm)

5804269 Hunter & Navy

Songbird Village® Plaid
Collection: Village® Home for the Weekend
Pattern #5808731 Navy
Other Colorways: Black, Hunter & Navy
Width: 20 1/2" (52cm)
Vertical Repeat: 2 1/4"

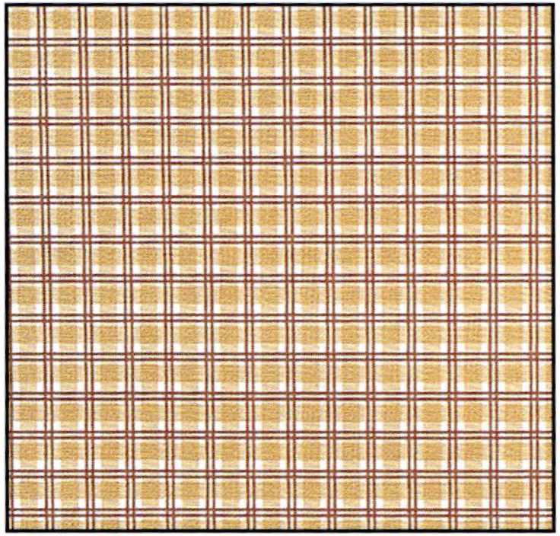

5812032 Ochre & Red

Woven Gingham
Collection: Village® Essential Kitchen and Bath 2
Pattern #5812031 Black & Sand
Other Colorways: Blue, Ochre & Red
Width: 20 1/2" (52cm)
Vertical Repeat: 2 1/8" (5cm)

Garden Linen Plaid

5806495 Sky

Garden Linen Plaid
Collection: Village® Toiles & Florals
Pattern #5806497 Dusty Rose
Other Colorways: Linen, Sky, Yellow
Width: 21" (53cm)
Vertical Repeat: 4 1/4" (11cm)

5806496 Linen

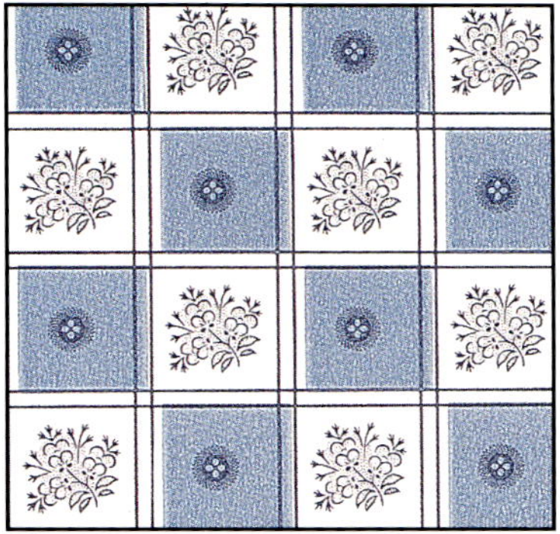

202790 Chambray

Greenwich Check
Collection: Greeff® Portraits of America
Pattern #202794 Sage
Other Colorways: Chambray, Coral, Buttercream, Golden Red, Beige & Green
Width: 27"
Vertical Repeat: 2 1/8"

202792 Golden Red

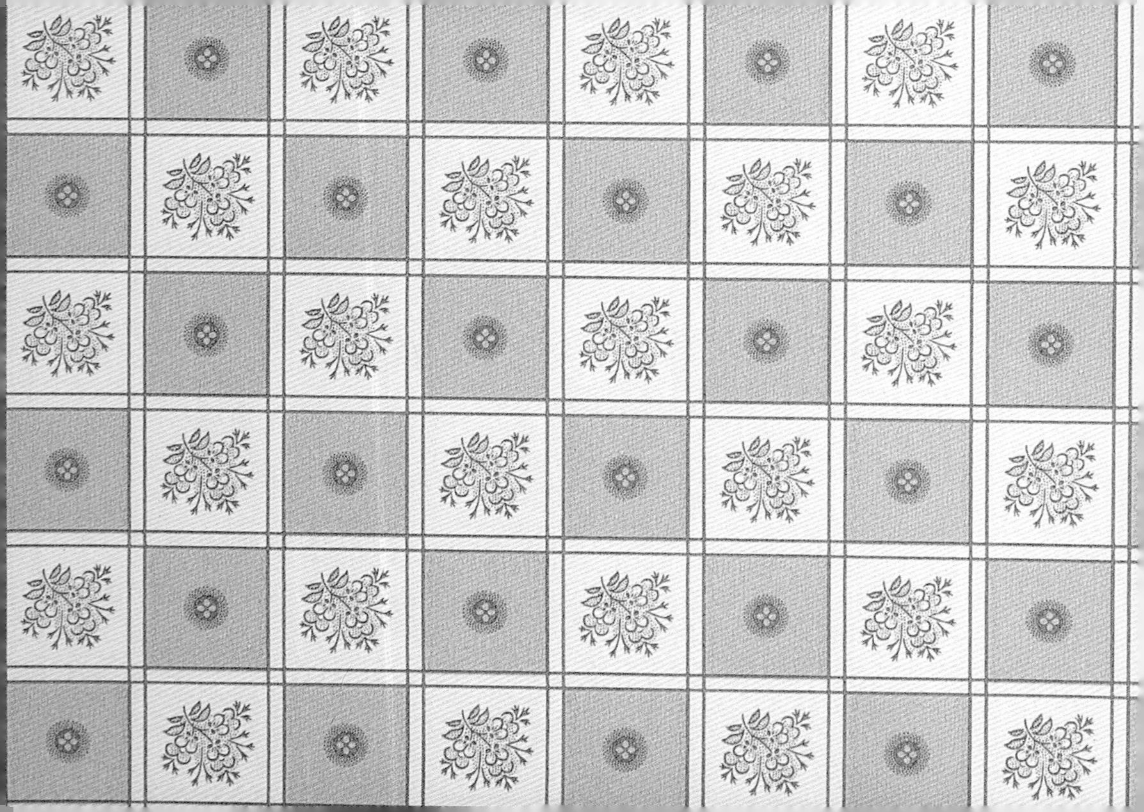

5502940 Country Red

Farmington Check
Collection: Waverly® Country House
Pattern #5502945 Black
Other Colorways: Country Red, Crimson, Tan, Evergreen, Slate
Width: 20 1/2" (52cm)
Vertical Repeat: 18" (45.72cm)

5502941 Slate

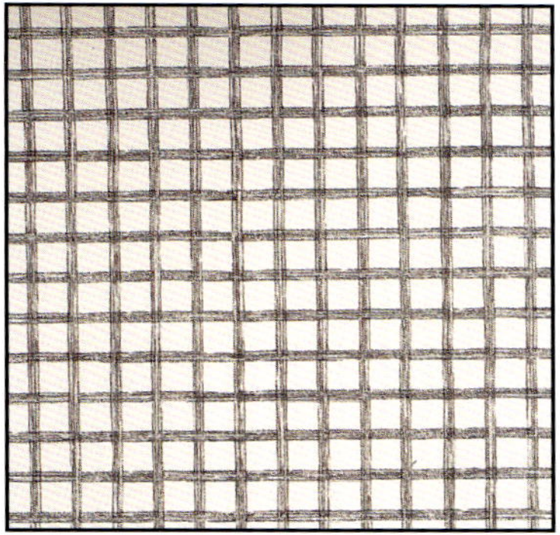

5810504 Black

Folk Art Grid
Collection: Village® Borders For All Around the Hous
Pattern #5810503 Country Red
Other Colorways: Navy, Maize, Forest, Black
Width: 20 1/2" (52cm)
Vertical Repeat: 10 1/4" (26cm)

5810501 Maize

591846 Denim & Ivory

Hopscotch
Collection: Village® Vintage Countryside
Pattern #591845 Brick & Honey
Other Colorways: Buttercup, Shetland, Beige, Denim & Ivory
Width: 20 1/2" (52cm)
Vertical Repeat: 5 1/8" (12.7cm)

5804771 Beige

Layers of patterns and fabrics create a collected country look. Shown: Waverly® American Landscape

Chickadee Trail
Collection: Waverly® American Landscape
Pattern # 5506992 Hunter
Other Colorways: Sage & Purple, Navy
Width: 20 1/2" (52cm)
Vertical Repeat: 10 1/2" (27cm)

Wallpaper, painted groove paneling, and chicken-inspired décor items create a cozy country theme in this foyer.
Shown: Waverly® Family Style

Folk Building Toss
Collection: Village® Country Style
Pattern #5810635 Beige
Other Colorways: Teastain & Burgundy, White
Width: 20 1/2" (52cm)
Vertical Repeat: 20 1/2" (52cm)

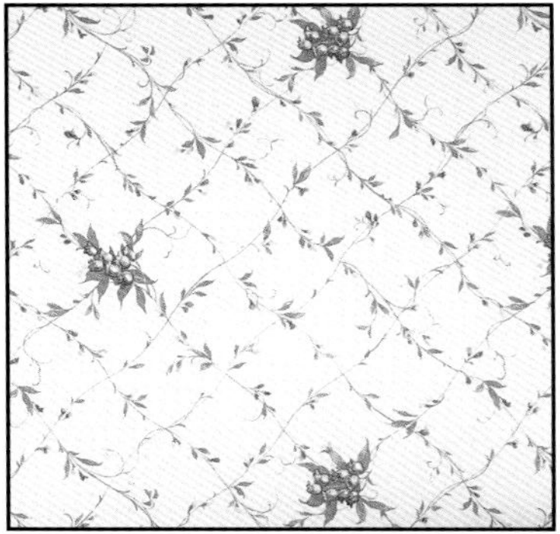

5505731 Blue

Melrose Trellis
Collection: Waverly® American Landscape
Pattern #5505730 Purple
Other Colorways: Blue, Yellow, Cream & Sage
Width: 20 1/2" (52cm)
Vertical Repeat: 20 1/2" (52cm)

5806528 Black

Daisy Trellis
Collection: Village® Toiles & Florals
Pattern #5806525 Red
Other Colorways: Black, Blue, Sage
Width: 21" (53cm)
Vertical Repeat: 2" (5cm)

A blue floral wallpaper pattern was used in the hallway to complement and add contrast to the pattern used in the kitchen.
Shown: Waverly® Family Style

Summer Garden Toss
Collection: Village® Borders For All Around the Hous
Pattern #5810486 Raspberry & White
Other Colorways: Rose & Cream
Width: 20 1/2" ( 52cm)
Vertical Repeat: 10 1/4" (26cm)

5503885 Navy

Hampton Toile
Collection: Waverly® American Landscape
Pattern #5503884 Cherry
Other Colorways: Navy, Ebony
Width: 20 1/2" (52cm)
Vertical Repeat: 21" (53cm)

5806226 Lavender

Victoria's Floral Border
Collection: Village® Country Club
Pattern #5806228 Navy
Other Colorways: Antique, Lavender, Pastel
Height: 8" (20cm)

5806227 Pastel

5810472 Beige

Botanical Bathtub Border
Collection: Village® Borders For All Around the House
Pattern #5810471 Green
Other Colorways: Yellow, Beige
Height: 6 1/2" (17cm)

Floral patterns are popular in bedrooms. Solid blocks of color provided by the bedding, curtains, and painted furniture accent the wallpaper.
Shown: Waverly® Family Style

Folk Animals Border
Collection: Village® Country Style
Pattern # 5810630 Navy
Other Colorways: Burgundy
Height: 7 1/2" (19cm)

Dark green floral wallpaper and border are complemented by a sage-colored pattern, which adds contrast.
Shown: Village® Orchard Border

Provence Rooster Trim Border
Collection: Village® Claire Murray Lifestyles
Pattern # 5808345 Green
Height: 4 7/8" (12cm)

Wallpaper that looks like an aged stone wall lends rustic ambience to this kitchen.
Shown:Gramercy® Tuscan Country Home

Piazza Cafe Ceiling
Collection: Gramercy® Tuscan Country Home
Pattern #685790 Gold
Other Colorways: Neutral, Tan
Width: 20 1/2" (52cm)
Vertical Repeat: 21" (53cm)

5503045 Sunshine

Country Stencil Border
Collection: Waverly® Country House
Pattern # 5503040 Blue
Colorways: Red, Country red, Slate, Indigo, Sunshine, Antique Gold, Canvas
Width: 5.5"
Vertical repeat: 5.5"

5503042 Country Red

5803453 Navy Green

Connor Plaid
Collection: Village® Country Canvas
Pattern #5803452 Antique
Other Colorways: Sage & Rust, Navy Green,
Burgundy & Green
Width: 20 1/2" (52cm)
Vertical Repeat: 2"

5803450 Burgundy & Green

SUMMER CHERRY BORDER

680311 Yellow

Summer Cherry Border
Collection: Gramercy® Spring Fair
Pattern #680310 Primary
Other Colorways: Yellow, Cream, Tea
Height: 6.25" (15.88cm)

680313 Tea

5505783 Red & White

Barrymore Border
Collection: Waverly® American Landscape
Pattern #5505781 Navy
Other Colorways: Burgundy & Tan, Black, Red & Whi
Height: 7.375"
Horizontal Repeat: 20.4"

5505782 Black

## Glenmere

Glenmere
Collection: Greeff® Country Manor
Pattern #1012045 Yellow
Other Colorways: Document, Red & Green, Plum & Olive, Spring
Width: 54"
Vertical Repeat: 16"

## Glenmere Stripe

Glenmere Stripe
Collection: Greeff® Country Manor
Pattern #200742 Spring
Other Colorways: Document, Plum & Olive, Yellow
Width: 27"
Vertical Repeat: 1 1/2"

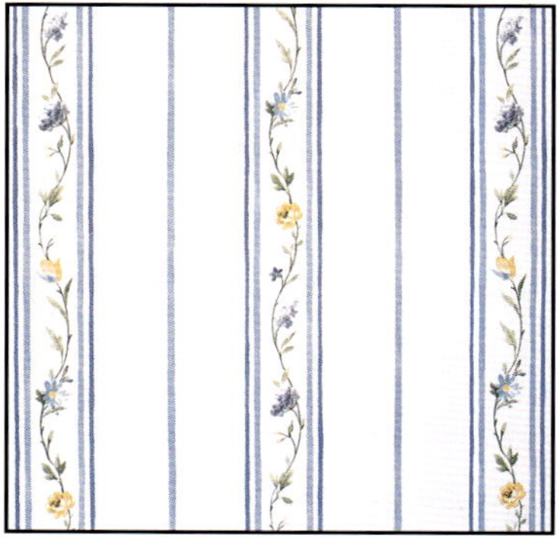

5503223 Blue & Yellow

Small Delights Stripe
Collection: Waverly® There's No Place Like Home
Pattern #5503224 Cream & Rose
Other Colorways: Blue & Yellow, Brights,
Purple & Sage, Plum
Width: 20 1/2" (52cm)
Vertical Repeat: 10 1/2" (27cm)

5810437 Black

Barnyard Buddies Border
Collection: Village® Borders For All Around the House
Pattern #5810436 Teastain
Other Colorways: Navy, Black
Height: 6 7/8" (17cm)

5503051 Antique

Country Quilt Border
Collection: Waverly® Country House
Pattern #5503050 Country Red
Other Colorways: Lake, Antique, Jewel, Thistle
Height: 5.625"

Cock-A-Doodle Doo Border

5811966 Black & Sand

Coc-A-Doodle-Doo Border
Collection: Village® Essential Kitchen and Bath 2
Pattern #5811967 Ochre & Red
Other Colorways: Blue & Sand, Black & Sand
Height: 7" (18cm)

5810360 Wedgewood

China Toile Border
Collection: Village® Borders For All Around the House
Pattern #5810361 Bleached Pine
Other Colorways: Wedgewood
Height 9" (23cm)

528652 Willow

Diamond Puff
Collection: Schumacher Blue Ribbon Collection
Pattern #528651 Camel
Other Colorways: Linen, Willow, Lacquer
Width: 27" (69cm)
Vertical Repeat: 1.8" (5cm)

528653 Lacquer

Fig. 11

548312 Red & Yellow

Aster Fruit Toile
Collection: Gramercy® Garden Elements
Pattern #548313 Black & White
Other Colorways: Red & White, Blue & White, Red & Yellow
Width: 27" (68.58cm)
Vertical Repeat: 25.25" (64.14cm)

548311 Blue & White

Chicken Wire Texture

Chicken Wire Texture
Collection: Village® Borders For All Around the House
Pattern #5810556 Teastain
Other Colorways: Parchment
Horizontal Repeat: 20.5" (52cm)
Vertical Repeat: 20.5" (52cm)

Rustic Farm Border

Rustic Farm Border
Collection: Village® Absolutely Vintage
Pattern #5812186 Burgundy
Other Colorways: Whitewash & Navy
Height: 7" (18cm)

5810615 Burgundy

Country Perch Border
Collection: Village® Country Style
Pattern # 5810618 Navy
Other Colorways: Burgundy, Yellow, Sky Blue
Height: 8 3/4" (22cm)

Diamond Dot Toss

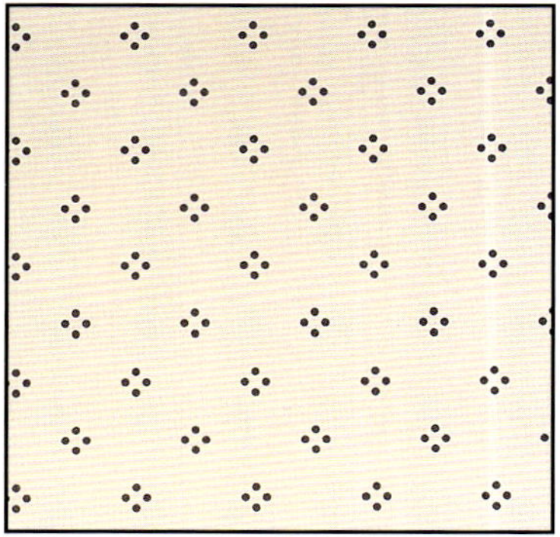

579526 Indigo

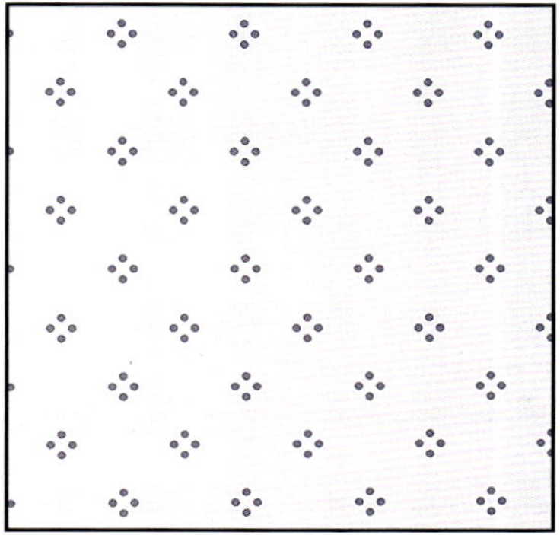

579525 Slate

Diamond Dot Toss
Collection: Waverly® Country House
Pattern #579524 Red
Other Colorways: Thistle, Blue, Slate, Indigo, Country Re
Crimson, Yellow, Pearl, Vintage
Width: 20 1/2" (52cm)
Vertical Repeat 10 1/4"

5806961 Chambray & Green

Americana Quilt Border
Collection: Village® Liberty Home
Pattern #5806962 Antique
Other Colorways: Chambray & Green, Traditional
Height: 6 1/2" (17cm)

5806960 Traditional

Heart Of America

Heart Of America
Collection: Village® Liberty Home
Pattern #5807016 Brights
Other Colorways: Antique, Teastain, Chambray & Rec
Width: 20 1/2" (52cm)
Vertical Repeat: 5 1/8" (13cm)

Heart Of America Border

Heart of America Border
Collection: Village® Liberty Home
Pattern #5807010 Brights
Other Colorways: Antique, Teastain
Height 6 1/2" (17cm)

5507023 Teal

Star Spangled Toss
Collection: Waverly® American Landscape
Pattern #5507022 Burgundy
Other Colorways: Sage, Navy, Teal
Width: 20 1/2" (52cm)
Vertical Repeat: 20 1/2" (52cm)

Create A patchwork of friendship with Love, kind

5807045 Teastain

Patchwork Trail Border
Collection: Village® Liberty Home
Pattern #5807046 Ecru
Other Colorways: Teastain
Height: 5" (13cm)

This fruity border adds color to a room rich in neutral tones.
Shown: Village® Vintage Countryside

Houndstooth
Collection: Waverly® Saratoga
Pattern #5507682 Coffee
Other Colorways: Parchment, Toffee
Width: 20 1/2" (52cm)
Vertical Repeat: 4 1/2" (11cm)